the hunchback

POEMS BY
SANDY DIAMOND

CREATIVE ARTS BOOK COMPANY
Berkeley • 2000

"Working at the Tasty Shop" first appeared in *Fireweed*.
"So I Was on Haight Street Today" appeared in
The Haight Ashbury Literary Journal in an earlier version.

Grateful acknowledgment to Centrum, Port Townsend, Washington where
much of this book was written as Poet-in-Residence.

The Hunchback is published by Donald S. Ellis
and distributed by Creative Arts Book Company

For information contact:
Creative Arts Book Company
833 Bancroft Way
Berkeley, California 94710

For ordering information call:
1-800-848-7789
Fax: 1-510-848-4844

Cover Art: Sandy Diamond,
"Flowered Ashtray and Snailshell," private collection

ISBN 0-88739-288-1
Library of Congress Catalog Number 00-101348

Printed in the United States of America

*this book is dedicated
to its loving critics,
the girlz on mt hood*

& to our comrade, Susan Spady
in memoriam

Contents

THE HUNCHBACK

WORKING AT THE TASTY SHOP

ZANZIBAR AND XANADU

THE HUNCHBACK

SMALL PEOPLE OF AMERICA:
A PRESS CONFERENCE

Baby carriers & backpacks have got to go.
Small people struck by baby feet & trailmix—
no more short end of the stick!

We don't blame the little urchins—children
are our natural allies, the *temporarily* short people
of America. We nudge them at spectacles & parades
to cry, *Hey, down in front, Mister—we can't see!*

We are not a bunch of complainers.
Lower the door knob! lower the mirrors!
the coat rack! the coin slot!
we won't be shortchanged!

To join us: you can't be over four-ten—
no bent knees nor slicked-down hair!

Mostly we tell tall people jokes.
No, we're not allowed to tell them
to non-members.

We are equal one night a month.
We don't have to look up look up look up.
We look straight into each others' eyes
& laugh our little heads off.

IDENTITY

Driver's license photos never look like you—
Smile—but if you're the hunchback, shrinking half
an inch a year (now three inches below the info
you declare, under oath— I hope you know that) &
studying the rearview mirror, you see the local papers:
"Nabbed for Impersonating Taller, Happier Midget,"
the neighbors smirking, *Who does she think she is?"*

Picture ID?—always that ingratiating smile, not you at all,
you never look that hopeful, except the one time it really matters,
when the red & blue lights flash & whirr behind you
& you pull over (remembering to signal) & flick off the radio—

> You're not supposed to sit there listening to the radio
> even while he's calling into headquarters. Anyway
> you need the time to think up excuses.
> And get your seat belt on.

> I always wanted to get stopped on my birthday
> 'cause he's looking right at your date of birth & would he
> say, *Hey, it's your birthday! I'm gonna tear this ticket
> right up!* Or would he say, *You'd think you'd know better
> by now, wouldn't you?*

(But what if you were caught with Elvis singing "Love Me
Tender" & the officier melts? But what if he's hung up
on the drug thing & never *forgave* Elvis?)

—& hide the salad you were eating with your fingers
& now when it's too late you wish you'd read that article
on The Psychology of Law Enforcement,
especially the sidebar of Do's & Don'ts.

Very soon now you will turn your fraudulent body
to fumble for proof of ownership & he will see
the hump. Will he think: *She's got enough troubles,*
& let you off with a stern warning? Or will he think:
Get these goddamn freaks off the road!
& throw the book at you?

They don't ask you to get out of the car, do they?
He wouldn't say, *This here says four nine*
& you don't look over four six to me.

His boots crunch on the shoulder gravel.
You're watching in the sideview mirror.
You roll down the window & smile & say,
What seems to be the trouble, Officier?

THE JOKE

You know the joke about the hunchbacked
woman & the man with a wooden eye?—

He stands at the mirror in his lonely room
& screws in his terrible eye.

She slips a blouse over her head—it catches
on the hump. She tries to tweak it off,

but she can't reach. She wriggles, curses,
knowing no one will dance with her anyway.

Desperate, they each go to the singles dance,
see each other, stare, wondering,

& he says, *Would you like to dance?*
And thrilled, she cries, *Would I?! would I?!*
& he cries, *Hunchback! hunchback!*

I loved that joke when my back was straight
and my dance card full.

Now I wish I'd been there—
I'd be the lady serving punch.

When they pick up their paper cups,
I spike the bowl with vodka.

Such small cups, I cry.
Drink that up and have another.

They smile to themselves, raise their wobbly cups
of altered punch to the space just left of each other.

The band's playing an old Glenn Miller tune.
I know how to dance the fox trot,

she blurts out too loud. He takes her cup,
slips it in his, (a strawberry slurping out),

and flips them into the trash
without even looking.

The fox trot, he says. *The fox trot?*
That's easy.

THE HUNCHBACK OF NOTRE DAME, 1939: A REVIEW

While the film is being shot, Hitler
marches into Czechoslovakia.
Charles Laughton, lashed, turns on the pillory,
his face inhuman, a monstrous
approximation of man. Around and slowly
around he goes as though he turns
from humanity and wants
no part of it.

Despite his saving the day
with the boiling oil we love to see
pouring on the Parisians storming
the cathedral door and the swinging rope
of rescue —(*Sanctuary! Sanctuary!*)
in the end Esmeralda rides off
with the handsome poet.

Victor Hugo didn't do happy endings.
Quasimodo leans on a gargoyle less grotesque
than he and delivers his last line—
Why wasn't I made of stone like thee?—
disappearing as the camera backs away
until he's indistinguishable
from the facade of Notre Dame.

The most triumphant scene for this reviewer—
where Laughton, the homliest of our great actors,
and Quasimodo are one—is when the hunchback
makes love to Esmeralda by ringing bell after bell,
(his beloveds). She covers her ears at the din.
Smiling his misshapen smile, he says,
*You wouldn't think there'd be anything else wrong
with me, but I'm deaf.*

Laughton rang the bells long after the director
meant to yell *Cut!* *I did it,* said the actor,
not for Esmeralda, but to warn the poor, poor world.

REFUGEES

Postage stamps are so tiny and each one tells a story.
Here is World Refugee Year, 1960, four cents.
An Art Deco family forms one silhouetted mass.
Their backs to us in the gray funnel of searchlights,
they face a distant rectangle of white.

A man, a child adjoining him, a woman (her dress
like the picture on Ladies' Rooms). The shape
of a baby in the crook of her arm creates a hump
on the left side of the would-be Americans.

The hunchback squints at the slump
of the infant she holds in her tongs.
You don't have to be perfect to come here, she says.
Not all of us already here are perfect.

But this family has a more glaring problem—
they have no feet. Their legs taper to a point,
an Art Deco motif. Well-dressed, close-knit,
but how far can they get, really?

Someone with a magnifying glass on his head
engraved this stamp. Maybe he was a refugee too.
Maybe he lost his family in another land.
He is making a new family.

Maybe he had a hunchbacked child. And this
was his chance to love it at taxpayers' expense.

We cannot see the baby's feet. Maybe
they're real feet and as soon as it can walk,
it will try to walk away from the hump
behind it. That's going to be one long walk.

Now we see the refugees are not just looking for
a better life—they want a better body for their child,
here in the land of opportunity
and Yankee know-how.

Forty years have past since they came
to The Promised Land.
The collector tucks the stamp back
into the protective sleeve of her album.

EXPRESSIONS

She wakes to the smell of smoke.
Listens for a rush of air and flame.
It would be a cross, burning in the garden.

Before she moved to the country,
friends said,
>   *You'll be the only Jew there.*
And who was she, small twisted one,
to represent her race?

She plucks back the shade to look for the red glow.
Once, a neighbor, talking about getting a part
for his truck, bragged to her,
>   *I really jewed him down.*

Suddenly tasting all her metal fillings, she said,
>   *I'm a Jew and it hurts me*
>   *when you say that.*

He stared at her. A Jew! Clearly his first.
She hoped her hair was neat. She wanted to explain:
>   *They're not all like me.*

He said,
>   *Hey, that's just an expression, see.*
>   *To you,* she said.
>   *It's just an expression to you.*
>   *To me, it's a dagger in the heart.*

Pearls of condensation jewel
the windowpane. Perfumed, the earth
is rising for another day. Birdsongs tumble
from old trees. The cross must be burning out,
she thinks—they start them
in the middle of the night, I'm told.

      Hebe, hymie, kike—
they're just expressions.

She lies in bed, sniffing.
The garden swells green and white with song.
The birds wouldn't do that,
she tells herself, if a cross were burning.
Does she smell smoke or not?
Maybe it's a phantom memory—
first cigarette, first beau, whispering,
      angelpie, lambikin, oh chickadee.

THE HUNCHBACK IN THE SUPERMARKET

Just my luck, it's a law of merchandising:
if it has a bird on it, it goes on the top shelf.
I wait for someone to come to my aisle.
Don't think I don't know everyone's avoiding
Condiments because a hunchback's lurking here.

The parrot on the label of my favorite sauce
watches me trying to reach him. I couldn't
reach him last week nor the week before, but
I make a big show of it, my fingers inching up
the fancy vinegars, just to keep him on his toes.

He grasps a branch, too stiff-necked
to see it's disconnected from the tree.
He thinks he's got a safe perch.

Insolent fowl! mouthing the grocer's classist rant:
top shelf, top shelf! You think because you can talk,
someone's going to listen? I got news for you,
Polly—no one's giving away any crackers.

Two teenagers, tall as longing,
levitate into my aisle. All dove & coo,
their hands in each others' back pockets
as though to hold themselves down to earth.

Effortlessly the lovebirds pluck the parrot
from the shelf, float it to my cart & lilt
to the end of the aisle. The frayed ends of
their cutoffs caress their thighs, reminding
them of each other at every step.

They're whispering by the Jams & Relishes.
Does he ask: *A hunchback—is that supposed to be*
good luck or bad luck? Good luck, she whispers,
but you have to touch the hump.

God knows I wish them luck.

MORTALITY

You are the hunchback.
You sit on a cushion for height and softness
when you drive. Your back bulges out
between the shoulders and flattens at the rear end
like a wrecked car buckles.
Still, though, you're recognizable
as a mortal vehicle.

Like those trucks with layers of flattened
cars with families once inside and the radio on—
Do we have to listen to that?—children
fighting over the armrest, the mother turning
the map upside down and the father
yelling, *Where* are *we?*

Now their Roadmasters are scrap
on the scrap heap and you know you'll never
have a curvy ass again nor be tall enough
to see where you are going,
yet when the truck of mashed steel
drives by, you cry, *Look at those cars!*

TRUCKIN'

Under the brawny sun-dark left arm
of the bigrig driver, rides the company's logo
in italic gilt—the last place in America you can find
a macho man associated with dainty script.

Propped up on her driving cushion, she looks
like anyone else. Her long hair blowing
gives the wrong impression. But to her,
she's the hunchback, exempt from pick-up games.
The trucker sees her looking at the writing
on his door & thinks her interest is him.

Once, driving the Siskyou Pass, she couldn't
get *Dick's Long Distance Hauling*—shadowed &
flourished—off her tail. Slowed down, sped up,
& she thought she'd lost him. Just when she opened
her mouth to eat a half-peeled banana,
the aesthetically endowed bigrig heaved alongside.

To the banana-loving trucker, her action meant
one thing. Going ape, he pursued her with gestures
suggesting how to shift gears. Horn blasting,
he blocked exits & every time he passed, his tongue
was out as if he meant to steer with it.

Seeing his logo so often, she realized the serifs
were weak. When a third lane appeared approaching
Sacramento, she hid between two eighteen-wheelers
with stencilled logos no one would look at twice.

CROSSING

On the curb, waiting for the light to change.
The hunchback's eye to eye with an eight-year-old
holding his mother's hand & staring.
The hunchback stares back.

Are you a child? he whispers.
Are you a peanut butter sandwich? she sez.
He chews on this, then sez, *Are you a pooky pokey pie?*
She curves her arms into a huge gorilla & sez,
Are you a hooga hunga munga bunga?

He giggles, the sign sez *Walk,*
the mother yanks him into the street & sez,
Don't laugh at funny people!

TWENTY YEARS

Sometimes she feels twenty years
older than she is. Shuffling into the front yard
in her Minnie Mouse slippers, she shakes
her stick at the traffic running by her house.

The bigrigs think she's signalling them
to blow their deafening airhorns & it's obvious to her
from the racket, mufflers are a thing of the past.

Why must you drive back & forth on God's
green acres? Why don't you stay put inside
like decent people? Slow down, you sons-of-bitches,
stop having so many babies! Can't you grasp the concept
that overpopulation is the devil! That's why so many cars are red
& your RV looks like a breadbox or a thermos!
If the sheriff had any balls, you'd all be in blindfolds,
smoking your last cigarette!

When her voice cracks like old, dry cheese, she minnies it
back to the house, feeling twenty years younger—
when traffic wasn't a menace
& no one saw it coming,
when traffic wasn't a menace
& no one saw it coming.

THE POOL

Short fast kicks ... big deep kicks ...
She hangs on to the edge below the instructor's call.
She wants Poseidon or Neptune to rise up
out of the deep end, triton dripping, and boom:
Your years of floundering are over. Go live
on dry land with your own kind.

Up   down   swing back   one ...
A bandaid swims across the painted blue lane,
tiny bubbles streaming from its air holes.
Somebody's thumb, she thinks, was cured
in this municipal water, healed
by its own hand, opening ... closing
like an anenome.

Up   down   swing back   two ...
She spies a long slender object wobbling
through the vapors, a u-curve on one end,
a rubber tip on the other.
She pretends she's snorkling in Hawaii. Snorkel
is an ugly word, suggesting swine—
she prefers to call it visionary aquatics.

Up   down   swing back   three ...
A glint of metal amidst the minnows and seaweed—
a wheelchair floats by, its foot rests
flapping like fins.

A dark shape bobs in the tide. *Up   down ...*
not another appliance, yet something must save her.
Lungs heaving, parched, she goes under,
rises, fits into its old ring: an inner tube, sun-
warmed rubber smelling of childhood.

Up   down   swing back   four ...
Lichen scuzzes the side of the pool where shore-
lines of tile have washed away. Drifting
past the four foot mark, above the transient floor,
her perfect feet trail in the water.

THE HUNCHBACK IN HER SHOWER

She draws the curtain. The song
begins. Reaches for the two white stars—
H and C—on the green tile walls that steam
and glisten. The stars know her temperature
by heart.

Water cantilevers off the hump.
Her soap's name is Pure & Natural, she buys it
for that reason. A tortoise-shell brush leans
in a corner—*faux,* of course, but she likes
the symbolism: slowness, the numbing
shield—to scrub oneself
with winning.

Flings her long hair under the spray.
Hair that peekaboo'd her breasts back then,
hair that hid her back which needed,
then, no hiding, her hair tangling in the fingers
of lovers as they sang out together, hair
parted like theater curtains on a night when
attendance was good.

The hair never mattered, it was the body—
reaches for the Fuller Body shampoo,
pours it in her hand, claps her hand to her head
as though she just remembered something—

Who would ever think her hair would
be this long and dark and thick and
shiny after all these years?

NOTHING BAD

At my family's restaurant, the refugees
wore humps inside their black coats. Bowed
over misty bowls of soup, they looked like a mountain range,
as though their journey were inside them.

A child, I imagined the displaced people flocked
at harbors where not enough boats would sail to America.
Since everyone had a number,
someone called out, *Hunchbacks first.*

All afternoon they sipped hot tea from a tall glass,
a lump of sugar held between the teeth.
And forever waved baskets for more braided rolls, more
challah, as though what manners they had over there
didn't come with them.

The waitresses knew not to give them the rush
even as Fanny, Blanche & Marge billowed & spread
the white tablecloths of dinner, hoping
the breeze would reach "The Old Country"
(as we called their pushed-together tables) & they'd take a hint.
But our little ghetto was beyond hints.

The one we named The Scholar always disputed his check
as though it were The Talmud.
Cashier, waitress & pedant stood poking their pencils
at the pale lined paper that still said *Thank you for coming.*
If anyone was going to be cheated,
it wouldn't be him.

They who bowed to my mother
famous for playing the emigré Chopin
like a dream.

Once the Old Country was up in arms
about the thickness of a blintz.
Mrs. V, the Hungarian cook, stormed out from
the kitchen & loomed over the grievance committee
staring up at her. As big as two chopping blocks
on piano legs, in such a huff she still held
her rolling pin, her apron vast & snowy
as Siberia, she clapped her mitten hands, producing
a magic puff of flour. *Shame on you!* she said.
She'd been through what they'd been through.

The noisiest perched on the aisle like a crow
plucking the ruffled aprons of waitresses flying by.
One time, holding an apple struedel, I swerved too close—
her sharp fingers caught my plump arm. *Look at this!* she cawed.
You better not criticize my daddy's pastry, I said in my mind
where I hoped she couldn't hear me. *Kenahora,* she said,
the other blackbirds nodding in a row, while I breathed again—
kenahora: nothing bad will happen.

Half a century later the restaurant's gone— Mother,
Father, Mrs. V, our crooked-back customers.
They would have been the first to go.
Their complaints about our incomparable borscht,
our *latkes* light as angels
seem to me now a ritual to keep
the ghosts of their dead from envy.

Did Nature armor them with humps
to stave off the thrusts of history? Or
did these humps spring full-fledged when a guard
tapped them on their bony backs,
grinning *Not yet.*

Do they store provisions there for crossing
their private Sinai's? Are such deformities meant
to be straightened? Are they not testaments, bulging
medals of grace, like bread rising misshapen
from the wrong recipe, the crooked
staff of life.

Ah Quasimodos of my parents' mercy,
let me be a girl again holding on to a sweet—
for who's to say a hump isn't a good thing,
all your pain knotted in one bundle
behind you, *kenahora.*

WORKING AT THE TASTY SHOP

BEDTIME STORY

Mother reads you a fairy tale,
stressing the difference between picking flowers
and picking every flower in sight.
That says something about you, she says.
*And anyway, you're under instructions
to go to Grandma's house.*

*But she wanted to give the flowers
to Grandma,* you say, knowing this is a lie.
And Mother says, *Don't kid yourself, kiddo—
Grandma doesn't have that many vases.*

You try to stay awake but your lids droop
like rain-dark trees. Your red Dr. Denton's
blur into a cloak, its hood thrown back
like a bright pool of dreaming.

Fragrance gathers heavy in your arms.
You remember Grandma.
Where did you put that basket of goodies?
You can't see over the heaped trilliums,
paintbrush, jacks-in-the-pulpit.
You can't see the path.

You are lost, kiddo—admit it
—weighed down and rooted in the woods,
your heady blooms wilting
like wrung necks.

A hush. The dappled shade. A tangle
of trunks. A sound in the underbrush—
as in a dream—not birds. Not squirrels.
It is the wolf, shifting on his haunches

as he studies hoodwinked you.
Slavering on the violets, he licks his chops
as he tastes you in his mind.
You let him get a whiff of you.
That's all it takes.

EDWARD G. ROBINSON

Is you is or is you ain't my baby? sings Daddy.
Mother looks like she wants to reach into his throat

and pluck the *ain'ts* out like tonsils.
You sound like a gangster, she says,

cold as a deepfreeze hung with meat.
And in front of the children.

Stick 'em up, he sez, his finger cocked at us,
and gimmee all yer cornflakes.

In the basement she prods the sheets with her mixingstick,
feeding them through the ringer which once caught

her little hand. Now the piano's for dusting.
The rollers can't squeeze the sheets
hard enough to suit her.

In the back yard, I'm Edward G. Robinson
locked in the slaughterhouse freezer by rival gangs.

I shadowbox with the slabs of beef to stay warm.
Youse, I say. *Youse lousy rat. You lowdown dirty rotten louse.*

*Youse ain't long for this world, youse ain't
no good. Youse ain't!*

Chanting in a circle under the animal stiffs, braids
unravelling, hands beating time in the air,

I don't see Mother out the back door, wet sheets cowering
in her basket, until she's in front of me screaming
my name. I look up—and for the first time
in my life, she slaps my face.

You're not my mother! You're not!
You ain't! You ain't my mother!
And I ain't your baby!

MOTEL

Things we'd done for years to save the Jews
we'd never do again: saving string and paper
and rubberbands. I was nine when we won The War.

Suddenly our tinfoil balls were worthless.
We wouldn't be turning them in
at the War Effort Saturday matinee any more.
That's when it was real to me The War was over.

The first winter of peace Ohio was just as cold
as it was during The War. That was the only
disappointment. But now we had gas and tires.
We'd never been anywhere before.
We drove to Miami Beach!

We had the world on a string—the zigzag line
of the spiral bound Trip Tik. My sister and I bet
on who'd turn the page as South Carolina
became Georgia, who'd get the most cows before
a cemetary. We cheered at all the state borders and
yelled out the messages on the Burma Shave signs.
Our boys had fought for our right to do this.

Sand'n Surf, Paradise Inn, Flamingo Hideaway.
Mottel, Dad said after each one, ruining everything.
Not "motel" like English, but *mottel* like Yiddish.
I thought this was a vacation! my sister cried.
You said we were leaving Cleveland behind!
Must we take Judaism to Florida?

Mom said, *Who do you think* lives *in Miami Beach?*
Jews! I yelled, just realizing it myself.
I too had thought we were going somewhere
utterly different from the life we had known.

1946

We're standing on the tracks
because the trolley won't stop at the synagogue.
The trolleyman hates Jews
even though The War is over.

A mile uphill to the bus terminal.
We're not walking, my brother says.
He's supposed to stop.
Our oxfords slip on the shiny rails.

I clutch my Hebrew books
which may not touch the ground.
If Hebrew touches the ground, Miss Zemetkin
says, you must pick up the twisting
black letters and kiss them.

5:10: The Jew-hater's trolley is right on time.
The rails' vibrations *wah wah* up my legs.
I'm shaking like those wooden dolls that dance a jig
when a stick hits by their feet, those do-
with-me-as-you-will shameless
puppets of shaking.

The spokes of the cowcatcher visible now—
how *dare* anyone make me die
when I'm reading *Jane Eyre,* when Miss Zemetkin said
my Hebrew script's the best in class, when overnight God
stuck two little pop-ups on my chest and I want
to know why and what other designs
He has on me.

The train is dangling from its overhead wire —
Blessed art Thou, King of the Universe...
Its clanging bells, the honking cars, blood
beating in my ears:
                    Stop now...
I see passengers gesture: Away!
                    God of Our Fathers ...
A woman's mouth opens:
a perfect o.
Black letters circle the train's iron face:
CLEVELAND TRANSIT SYSTEM, the last words
I'll ever read — oh *Jane!*

Hear O Israel ... The trolleyman's face
masked in the glare of the sun
setting on his windshield.
The one-eyed light will shine on our bodies
torn from their spines. *Then* who
will pick them up and kiss them,
Oh Holy One?

The trolley — screeching —grinds to a halt
fifteen feet away. My brother pulls me up
the stair, drops our fares in the box,
not looking at the trolleyman.

But *I* look. He stares straight ahead
as though we were still out there,
waiting for the 5:10
on the tracks of the Lord.

THE FIRE

Hatikvah Synagogue burned down, don't ask how.
Saved: the Torahs and books, everything else—*kaput.*
Hebrew classes continued in temporary barracks.

Hebrew looks like black flames far away,
like tongues writhing. Fitting that a language—
something you say—looks like tongues.
The letters hang from their tops like black socks
pinned to the clothesline. The most beautiful letter,
the *shin,* is a fiery three-pronged crown.
Some letters hold dots in their bellies
like embers. An incendiary's alphabet.

To remind you to open the workbook
from the Hebrew side, on the right-hand cover
an old man gazed in profile, his single eye
heavy-lidded from study.
The child wishes he'd turn toward her and say,
Your letters are a credit to our people.
Don't think God hasn't noticed.

One day a boy accidently knocked his workbook
to the floor. *Kiss that book!* the teacher cried.
How could their pencilled alphabets
matter so much? But they took her word for it.

The next class before the teacher came in,
a boy named Myron inched his book to the edge
of his desk and let it drop. *Oh my God,* he cried,
forgive me Abraham, Isaac and Jacob!
He picked the book up, pressed it to his lips
and kissed the old man with a smack.

The teacher entered smelling a rat.
Miss Zemetkin had straight ginger hair clasped
in a hopeful bun, round rimless glasses
magnifying her eyes, and an accent that spoke
of other worlds. Sacrilege reeked
from the writings arms of nine yellow desks.

She walked to the barracks window.
Wooden planks over charred ground.
Behind her back, the class froze except for
their eyes darting like tadpoles—
was someone coming to take Myron away?

At last she turned, her voice far away.
Put down your pencils, children.
Today we'll write with crayons.
You may use two or three colors
on the same letter, no black at all.

WORKING AT THE TASTY SHOP

The Ohio summer I turned
sixteen, I worked in my father's deli—
no longer one child out of four, I was
the soda jerk, the fountain girl, thrilling
names of my new identity.
In between shakes and banana
splits, *my speciality*, I served
coffee & quips like the real
waitresses, swayed in a business-
like manner like the real waitresses
so the whole counter leaned forward
to watch & one day when my back
was turned the delivery boy whacked
my behind with a huge loaf of rye—
o warm from the oven—infusing me
with steamy smells, piercing my heart
with caraway seeds—I felt like butter
melting—& famished I thought
as I grabbed for the whirling bread:
now   now I am beginning to live

COUNTERMAN

A pound of tongue.
Is the chopped liver fresh?
Customers line up at Take-Out.

How's your mishpochah? the silver-haired
counterman asks the department store girls, all *shiksahs.*

What's that?

You don't know what a mishpochah *is?* He feigns disbelief.
Smart girls like you? You better find out or
you're in big trouble.

Aw go on, you're teasing.

Listen honey, I'm old enough to be your father.
(He's old enough to be her grandfather.)
Every girl's got a mishpochah — *if not,*
wagging a finger at them, *oy what a life.*

They're all giggling by now.

A laughing matter it's not, cutie pies, I'm telling you.

I'm ringing up checks, huffy with indignation.
What if this *mishpochah* of his is a dirty word and
he's cooking the goose of my family's business?
And if it *is* a bad word, how can I ask anyone
what it means?

Although the wise-cracking counterman
was like an uncle to me, I was afraid of him.
Sleeves rolled up, the bluish numbers blurred on his arm
as he made the best sandwiches between Chicago and New York.

When I checked him out at five, he hung around
my candy counter, straightening the gum —
the toothpicks even — turning the two-cent mints
right side up. *Go already,* I said in my mind,
you think this is home?

Finally one day after lunch, I marched
to the deli counter, leaned over the showcase of meats
and said in my boss's daughter voice, *Irving,*
I think you better tell me what a mishpochah *is,*
no joking around.

The old man put down his knife.
He wiped his hands on his apron of smears.
 Aiee, he said, *you don't know any Yiddish?*
 Your parents taught you nothing?

He began polishing the shiny bread slicer.
In a voice soft as mayonnaise he said,
 Mishpochah, *for your information, is family.*

TAFFETA

At twelve, the hunchback-in-waiting
was considered civilized enough
to go to the opera with her parents.
When she realized Pinkerton never intended
to marry Madame Butterfly, yet would take
the child, she clutched her mother's
taffeta arm and cried, *No!*

Then Madame Butterfly kissed the sword.
The girl felt cleft in two—half of her gladly
dying for love, the other half wishing
she'd stayed home with the babysitter.

Now five decades later, *Madame Butterfly*
is on the radio. Now that dying for love
is out of the question. No one even *wears*
taffeta any more. Can she bear to strain for
the sight of his ship again, knowing
what she knows? Pointing, murmuring
to the child: *Now, now, darling, he comes,*
while the plum blossoms at the heart
of her gown crash to the ground.

TRAVELOGUE

One teenage summer I had three steady beaus—
F, R and R. Both R's were friends of F
although the two R's didn't know each other.
This chance system of cross-reference
encouraged decorum all around.

Dubious meanwhile, Mother perched
on the upstairs landing, while at the door, F,
R or R applied the good-night kiss.
One evening as I floated up the stairs—exotic
from the explorations of an R—Mother
accosted me like a pesky beggar
from a foreign land. *How,* she hissed,

*can you kiss three different lips
in as many days?* I knew she wasn't asking
for advice. *Perhaps*—her eyebrows arched
like the interior of some medieval church—
your father should install a revolving door.

Mother sat with me on my frilly bed.
A girl's body—she chose her words
like tidbits on a doilied tray a fly
had lit upon—*is like the Promised Land.
Boys, born to poach, are cursed with wander-
lust. At best you are to them a tourist
attraction. Girls need a fixed address.*

I lie alone in my no-frills bed. She visits
me in dreams. I'm in the back seat
of her Dodge, she's in front facing me.
F and R are past recall, though God knows
I would have loved a revolving door.
Let's go for a spin! she cries, driving faster
than real life—windows open, our long hair
flying full-length like two wild animals
hot on our trail.

DELICATESSEN

Young & hungry in California, we
brought home chopped liver from Tasty
Take-Out. Famished, we squeezed too hard & the filling
squirmed from the bread to our laps, maddening us
with passion & we ran with the food
to the bed which back then was a chunk of foam
covered in paisley.

The design of paisley suggests
primitive life forms wriggling toward each other &
it was California & we loved
chopped liver & it was the last time
our bodies would ever be so delectable.

Three decades later, paisley's back in style.
And a caraway seed stuck in the teeth
still recalls that longpast midnight snack. In fact,
the mere phrase *midnight snack* takes me back
to the paisleyed foam in that California flat:

oh the cat clawed at the door
& the ants were thick as flies
& we hid our only sheets in the trash
& we swore not to tell, lest our mothers find out
& scold us for wasting food our fathers worked so hard
to put on the table — on the *table,* mind you. Mind?
what mind? — we were chopped liver!

& we didn't care who had more pickle
or that they left the napkins out
& the cole slaw smelled suspicious
& the frilly-headed toothpicks
& the olives slick ball bearings—

though we knew that for *real* egg creams
it has to be New York,
we felt we'd got our money's worth

'cause they never hold the mayo
in the delicatessen of love.

.

ZANZIBAR & XANADU

kerouac

for Karen

crazy howie whacks our lower eastside fiveflight walkup
    grab yer shabby bebop armynavysurplus hipster hepcat pea coats
        someone wansta meetcha   we're all too happy
blond botticelli carolina me dark braids since firstgrade
    what time is it mister fox snap past tenement wino storefront
starving artists who can't stand it anymore
                            & eat their still lifes

& now you ask me where was it exactly what alley crossroad
    cul de sac tarmac switchback & i can't remember don't
even know if howie told us who it was we were
breathless wingfoot whizzbang going to see
                  (our compass the mapmaker:) like

god hisself sitting on a bed somewhere near first & a
    looking oh handsome as a pinup pinned to the wall of our
generation & howie offers us to him like how you'd offer a bowl
    of fruit miss nothin'-could-be-finer first of course he gives her
the once-over then me the fig the last thing
    you'd reach for so gently i didn't know what was coming
he lifts   my braid to his mouth
                & kisses it

he who died without tenderness & now i am old woman mending
    the truth & you want to know if it was the left braid or
the right. it was december 1958 i know that much because i
    wrote it down by february i'd be in my first asylum
where they wanted to know why i broke the neck off a bottle of
    turpentine daring the walls to come any closer oh carolina calling
the cops & on my little lunatic's cot kerouac
                    lifted my braid

& in the asylum of zombie injections they wanted to know why
    i had a knife collection & tried to burn
the house down (that couldn't have been me they were
    talking about) & it was midnight i was on the narrow rack
he jacked me up thru quicksand jaws of thorazine—

                                        snap out of it
pleads papa mama against new york in the first place
    her rat-tailed comb carving childhood's part down the center
of my skull & the nurse snaps *cut it why don't you?*
    why don't you just
                        cut it off?

he chose me somewhere between first & a yes above venus
    glist'ning on the half shell did he know
i was about to lose my only mind? *this happened*
    ask howie ask carolina (if you can find them) he raised
the right braid or the left like this
                        to his sal paradise lips

THE COPS

for Dianne

I sent my sister the poem where I say someone called the cops.
I tell her I just needed to say that for the poem—
no one ever called the cops on me despite everything.

But they did call the cops, she says.
I remember because you were waving a gun around
& yelling 'get Dianne out of here' & they called
Aunt Ruth to come & get me & then they called the cops.

I start to cry. I don't remember. She's got it wrong.
You were holed up in the dining room, she says

& I see the dark jungle wallpaper from the 50's remodel
which I blame for all my fear of change—the slashed green
flesh of philodendron, anthurium's cocky red poker
splashed on all four walls   at regular intervals.

They couldn't have had too many manic episodes
in our small town. It wasn't like a city where nuts are
everywhere. My parents had a certain reputation.

The jungle was between the breakfast room &
the hall. There were two doors. I barricaded myself in,
forgetting that the door to the breakfast room was
a swinging door. They opened it   inch by inch
with their bare fingers & peered at me, their shiny
buckles glancing off the mirrored push plate.

Afterwards the officers apologized
for tracking in the snow.
They would have been low-key.
I was locked into my big moment.
I might never have a chance like this again.

BASEBALL

It's July 1965, month of the bodycast.
It's too tight, I accuse the doctors—
smug dressmakers, I the dummy—
You don't know how to measure.

This was Psychiatric, body &
soul finally together—broken.

There's this kid on the ward, sixteen.
He has this mother, a looker in tight sweaters.
That's his problem right there.
The whole floor hears him scream, hurl & thud
against the walls. The attendant comes trotting,
his restraining device of buckles & straps.
Slut! we scream at the looker in our minds.

There is a dress code for visiting the disturbed.

Me, I'm all decked out in plaster.
The kid trusts me because I have no apparent
body. We're both crazy about baseball. Feller Rosen
Lou Boudreau. The concepts of spring training,
taking the full count, sliding home.We swear
when we get out we'll only go for the long one.
Neither of us is into sacrifice.

Meanwhile, sneaky in the dugout of my healing,
the parts of bone reach out for each other.

I tell him about 1954 when we won the pennant.
I make it even better than it was so he won't leave me
when the cast comes off.

They never tell you what happened to the others—
this is in the interest of sanity.

Is he crowding the plate.
Is he running backwards in the sun
arms up, crying, *It's mine!*

That is not him, holding his head at the end
of the bench, hands taped. The bleachers
empty, except for a few ragtag homeless
picking through the red & white checkered
paper boats in hopes of a piece of something
still left from yesterday's game.

DRUGSTORE PAIN PILLS

in their cotton-stoppered vials:
blue as the vein of your wrist,
white as a coma, or liver-colored
to make you think your healing
is already inside you.

Talk to them, pretty messengers
of deliverance. Say: *What a snazzy*
label you have. And your row is so neat.
(If it isn't, straighten it.)

Sometimes people shake them and
put them down in the wrong place.
Ten ninety-five! they scream.

When you change brands, don't cry out:
Lozenges! I expected round!
Criticism of a condition beyond its control
is bitter for a pill to swallow.

Reminisce with them
in the pharmacies of their pain.
Pills love to hear how an ancestor of theirs
cured your gout or migraine.

It's best not to mention the time (long ago)
you washed down a bottle of aspirin with Coke.
Talk of stomach pumps is like death to them.
They feel responsible and they're not.

MY MOTHER'S KITCHEN

*Cut for me this up, you should be
so kind.* Lately a tremor seizes her hand.
I chop onions.

Get a load of this one—she's waving
the temple bulletin: "Births"—
*Christina Cohen. That's a name?
Anne Frank they all should be*—*that
by me's a name. Boys too,
it wouldn't kill them.*

But how could you tell anyone apart?

*What good did being apart do?
Better they should all be one.*

Salt, syrup, peanut butter, the box
of Constant Comment—all must be
turned so the bar codes don't show.
They remind me of you know what.

I take down the baking soda.
She pushes the row of boxes, closing
the gap. *Ma, I'm going to put it
right back.*

Holes I don't like.

Tell my mother's kitchen The War
is over. Tell Peter Pan in his tattered
green dress, the girl caught
in the rain—when it rains it pours—
thank God an umbrella.

I pry open the old space
for the baking soda, its strong arm
back home next to the boy and
his dog who live in the log cabin of sweetness.

THE EXHIBIT

1.

My job is to record attendance.
I push a button on my counter
each time someone enters.

2.

Not so easy as you'd think—
people come and go and come back.
I have no one to ask how to handle this.

3.

Or a group will surge past the Historical
Context without looking, spreading out
to the flashier displays where they disappear
into the already counted.

4.

Now a busload of children.
The first thing they see is the yellow star,
threads once sewn to someone's coat
still hanging like tiny stick figures.

5.

I detain them and their teachers
while I secure an unassailable count.

6.

The children examine the bits of costume.
They love every piece of information
they can get about Anne Frank.
It's as though she were a chum of theirs
who had a great adventure.

7.

They watch the movie of the Diary.
Anne Frank erases the answers
to her crossword puzzle,
gives it to Mother as a gift. They continue
this practice back and forth, until Year Two,
when the paper finally tears.

8.

When the children come to the Camp section,
they spot the numbers right away.
The photographs are hard to read,
but they stick with it, saying, *That's a three—no,
it's an eight!* They make up a little game:
who can find the highest number.

ON MY RADIO

The famine in ... click.
Shallow graves reveal ... click.
Amnesty International ... click.

I want them to warn us—play
a theme song for the horror ahead
like music from the shower scene of *Psycho.*

Now the radio itself bulges with bad news.
The plastic box crawls as though to get away
from the source of sorrow.
Ladybugs are falling from the window's lips
onto the radio. Their gauzy wings
flutter but don't lift them.
Their round red backs turn amber
as they die. The radio
is heaped with their tiny dry bodies—
ladybugs from nursery rhymes
falling to the shelf, to the floor.

I don't know what to do.

Each time one hits the plastic,
there's a little clicking sound.

BURNING THE WASTEBASKET OF CALLIGRAPHY

Once I was happy lettering
songs, poems, ascenders, descenders,
the voluptuous g, serifs & arabesques:
Hebrew, Uncial, Gothic, Legend.

Remember holding paper
up to the light, the felicity of
watermarks, a ram's head, a griffin,
a hand holding

a star? A page of *bliss* in brushscript,
a sheet of ampersands
scroll their wheelchairs on the heels
of bliss into the glow.

Pen scratches — spirals, hairlines,
loops — groping for the proper flow
of ink. Texture & text
embrace, sift, die.
Now a drift of tracing paper

— to track the flight of alphabets —
flutters to the fire, pencilled
margins slump in a puff of burnt umber,
the last scrap shudders & sighs
like a woman as the heat
licks through.

ZANZIBAR & XANADU

Her weathered sign at the campus crafts fair says:
GRAPHOLOGY: Good Enough for Aristotle, Shakespeare
& Emerson. Who You Are: five dollars.
Who You Can Be: ten.

Students line up to write the sentence
devised to reveal their secret selves:

Cruising with poets & mystics,
few visits to Zanzibar & Xanadu
were more joke than quest.

Because of X, Z & the ampersand, she has them
write it three times. While they fidget with doubt &
a longing for greatness, she devours the page,
hungry for signs of "the genius g."

Everything counts.
The margins, the pressure,
the space between lines,

the space between words,
between letters.
Rhythm. Size. Slant.
Departure from a straight line.

Hey stud, why are all these bananas
below the line? How 'bout some energy up here
in the spiritual realm for a change?

She says: *See here, young man, your ascenders*
& descenders are all in a tangle. Sure Beethoven
did it but so do madmen. If I were you,
I'd go for the second five bucks.

And once, the plunging lines of the would-be
suicide sliding down the page.
She says: *This is our only cruise, my dear—*
we all have to sail. Lasso your t's (like this)
for persistence. Dot your i's like birds flying.

Take this fresh paper, your ocean. Your only life
longs for you. How dare you die now
when you've never seen Zanzibar?

AT THE WOMEN'S CORRECTIONAL CENTER

I already *know* how
to write **Visitors shall
wear** I'm good **conventional
clothing** *really* good **not unduly
suggestive** What I really want
or tight-fitting is to be
published **No halter tops or see-
through sheer fabrics loose weave**
The world out there **Wearing
underclothes** needs to hear
is required what I have to say **Ex-
posing an undue amount of flesh**
It's written down I tell you
shall not be allowed I could
give it to you **No physical
contact** You could give it to a
publisher **except a brief embrace**
You are out there **and kiss
upon meeting and leaving.**

MAKING PROGRESS

Not being a finalist
for the book awards
takes me back thirty years
to the mental hospital.
The nurses would say,
Yes, you are getting
better, you'll be out
any day now, winking
to each other and rolling
their eyes to heaven.

THE THREE OF US

Curly had a big day, didn'tcha.
He swam in the riverton—
he's a swimmerboy.
He chased Whiskers and Pufferball—
big doggerboy. He says,
I'm a handsome doggerton, Daddy.

I'm working in the garden and fetcherboy
stood two inches from Daddy's elbow
all morning waiting for someone to throw
the stickerton. He ran like a deer
and made Daddy laugh. Didn'tcha.

Like how we laughed with Ted.
We don't mention T E D much anymore
'cause Curly gets that look in his eye.
He remembers. Don'tcha.
Come up here—oh he knows
he's a lapperboy.

We ran along the beach—Laguna,
Nantucket, the three of us. Remember
how you were snuggertons in bed
between us. Remember when
you'd lie on Ted's feet, warm loverboy
on Ted's cold white feet.

He'd say, *Put Curly up here, I have to
turn.* I'd lift you to his side and he'd face
a different window. Then you'd creep-
ertons back down to his feet. As if you
could keep him there. Didn'tcha.

SO I WAS ON HAIGHT STREET TODAY

for James M

I didn't mean to look for you.
The shops are impossible now, my dear—
not what you knew.

I thought I glimpsed the veiled hat,
blond wig—your own hair disappearing
by then—you wore to that last party
when a flowered teacup
trembled in my lap.

Haight Street is flimsier
without you, less witty. Where is
your butler's *hauteur* that might have
kept the standards up?

Last week in the park near the oleander
someone held a gun to William's head.
As soon as his pockets were empty
he ran and didn't look back.

You went so fast, with all your grace intact.
You are considered among the lucky ones.
This is what luck has come down to.

On the last day you said, *I wish
I could walk down Haight Street once more.*
But I think if there is any justice
in the world, you left in time.
This is what justice has come down to.

WHEN YOU ARE OLD

a line forms from the corners
of your mouth to your chin
until you look like a
ventriloquist's dummy.

And someone else
is always speaking for you—
Good evening, madam, you'll want
the Senior Special: creamed stew
with softened potatoes
& prune fluff—

while inside, you're eight years old
yukking it up with Charlie McCarthy
& watching Edgar Bergen's lips
like a hawk.

THE MAN WHO HUMMED TCHAIKOVSKY ON HIS DEATHBED

Not a line in his face, the eyes as blue as ever.
The hand he lifts looks like always
on an arm we don't recognize.
He beats his thumb on the metal side of the bed
how he used to on the breakfastroom table,
correcting our manners.

What's the song, Daddy?
Waltz ... he says, taking his time,
of The Flowers.

My sister and I hum the ballet,
amazed we know it.
We belt out the songs from family trips, Ohio
scrolling by like rollers on my childhood
blackboard. At *Down by The Old Mill Stream,*
he joins in, his dying
voice another kind of music.

The nurses pause in the doorway—
they didn't know he had it in him.

I ease the swollen feet which once we rode
up the goodnight stairs.
Mother ran the bath and knew
which play when he recited *Sleep*
with leaden legs and batty wings doth creep.
We thought he *was* Shakespeare.

Love letters in the candy box, 1929.
Sweetest Pal, Girl of My Dreams.
Today I fished in Lovesick Lake. Each line of script
flows to the edge of the page as though no time
to lift the pen, as though handwriting itself
would woo her, the high looped ascenders
of desire.

THE LAST POEM WAS ABOUT THE SOUL

We were critiquing at the diningroom table
when Jessica, the youngest, said, *Let's move
to the livingroom for the last poem.*
And everyone sat on the pillowed floor and
someone dragged my chair over and Jessica
flung herself full-length on the rug.

And her length was very full indeed, she stretched—
in my eyes—across the whole room
with its arched opening harem girls
with aquamarine navels might slink through.
And colored lights twinkled festooned
on the January walls as though a child
had drawn them there and the grown-ups
couldn't bear to say, *Christmas is over.*

And I wondered how many poems Jessica—
coltish, dreamy, smouldering—had sat through
on the stiff diningroom chair wanting to say, *Let's
move ...* so the length of her could lengthen,
her curls arabesque to the rug, its turquoise
a lagoon where the poem swam
toward its raft of meaning.

And I floated in and out of the poem's
arched windows—three, four decades ago to when
I knew how to arch and slink and fling, how to
enter a room and make the lights go on and off.

In the poem the soul is compared to
a cathedral and Jessica or someone said,
Do we need this architecture?
And I saw myself lying outside somewhere,
in a yard or a field, in my supple body I thought
would last as long as my everlasting soul.

Sandy Diamond's first book of poetry, *Miss Coffin & Mrs. Blood: Poems of Art & Madness* (Creative Arts Book Company, 1994) a finalist for the Pacific Northwest Booksellers Association Poetry Award, was produced as a staged reading directed by Penny Metropulos, New Plays Festival of Ashland, Oregon, 1995. She is the recipient of an Oregon Literary Arts Writing Fellowship for Poetry. Sandy Diamond lives in Port Townsend, Washington where she is currently working on her first play, *The Last Piece of Sky.* She performs her poetry with a jazz/blues band: "Quasimodo & The Bellringers."